LIGHT ARMOUR

LIGHT

ARMOUR

PLAYFUL POEMS ON
PRACTICALLY EVERYTHING

by RICHARD ARMOUR

Illustrations by
Leo Hershfield

McGraw-Hill Book Company

New York • St. Louis • San Francisco • Düsseldorf • Kuala Lumpur
Mexico • Montreal • Panama • Rio de Janeiro • Sydney • Toronto

The poems MAKE-UP ARTISTS (1945), MODEL HOME (1948), LINES LONG AFTER POPE, BY A READER OF FRESHMAN THEMES (1950), and PHILOSOPHY OF A LATE RISER (1952), were originally copyrighted in the respective years shown by The New Yorker Magazine, Inc.

Library of Congress Catalog Card Number: 54-9705

First McGraw-Hill Paperback Edition, 1971

07-002299-2

ACKNOWLEDGMENTS

Most of these verses first appeared in *The Atlantic Monthly, The American Legion Magazine, Better Homes and Gardens, The Christian Science Monitor, Collier's, Cosmopolitan, Country Gentleman, D.A.C. News, Esquire, Everywoman's, Family Circle, The Georgia Review, Good Housekeeping, Household, The New Leader, The New Yorker, The New York Times Magazine, New York Herald Tribune, The Pacific Spectator, Postgraduate Medicine, Quote, The Reader's Digest, Redbook, The Saturday Evening Post, The Saturday Review, This Week, Today's Health, Today's Woman, Town Journal, U.S.A., Westways, The Wall Street Journal,* and *Woman's Home Companion.* I am grateful to the editors and publishers for permission to use them in this volume.

To

KATHLEEN

For all I whimper,
Scold, and scoff,
I know that, wife-wise,
I'm well off.

PREFACE

Once upon a time a magazine editor asked me whether I could write a "long, thin poem." He explained that he wanted to fit it into a narrow column between two brassière advertisements. I replied immediately, which is a good way to reply to editors, saying that I was a long, thin poet, and therefore just the man for him, and that if he wanted a poem with a hole in the center to take up the slack in a doughnut ad, I could write one of those too.

There are some long, thin poems in this book, some short, fat ones, and some (for my middle-aged friends) that are narrow in certain places and broad in others. If a few poems are round, it is because they were written for circulars. But the shape of the poem, interesting and significant as it may be, is not of primary importance. Some of these poems have a Meaning. Others have a Hidden Meaning, and may have to be read twice. Such poems make the book more valuable; that is, they make it last twice as long.

Most of the poems in this book, however, can be readily understood, which is why they are not poems at all and why I should apologize for the use of the term. Actually this is a book of light verse. Years ago I wrote serious poems and was as morbid as anybody. If I had continued, I might now be required in school, like Longfellow. Or I might be a British citizen, like T. S. Eliot. Or I might be dead, like all the poets who really amount to anything.

But I switched over to light verse to avoid the competition. Everybody writes poetry. Relatively few, not more than ninety per cent of the population, write light verse. Besides I was tired of elevating my thoughts and keeping my brow high.

There are no Elevated Thoughts in this book. There are no really low thoughts either, because I should like this book to be sold in New England, and available in libraries without asking for the key. But I remember once, at a Chamber of Commerce banquet, reading some poems of mine to what seemed a very receptive audience and yet being cut off the air because of complaints telephoned in to the broadcasting station. I had always considered myself a Family Poet, and this incident continues to baffle me.

I like to read a new piece as soon as I have written it. If I am at home, I read it to my wife, who is usually vacuuming. When we were first married, she turned the vacuum cleaner off. Sometimes she turns the vacuum cleaner off now, but only because she has finished a room or is at the end of the cord. Demosthenes became a great orator by speaking with his mouth full of pebbles, and I am developing a certain resonance of tone by competing with a vacuum cleaner.

My wife is an excellent critic. She usually dislikes whatever I write, and tells me so. I would have quit writing years ago if I had listened to her. My children, on the other hand, like everything I write, especially when they are about to ask me for something I know they shouldn't have. Often I read my poems to people who pay to hear me. This is a good arrangement for everyone.

Light verse is a form of satire. The satirist, I find, is a misunderstood man. He is thought to dislike what he makes fun of. As a matter of fact, most of the things he makes fun of are what he likes most, such as his wife, his children, his friends, his dog, and himself. He makes fun of them because he knows them best and has discovered their wonderful oddities and inconsistencies. I have had neighbors, unfamiliar with this simple truth, who felt so sorry for my wife that they stopped speaking to me. It is unfortunate for a light-verse writer when people stop speaking to him, since it is from what people say that he gets most of his ideas.

Once I wrote a poem in which, in a playful sort of way, I wished someone dead. The editor to whom I sent the poem liked it but said it was against the policy of his magazine to publish anything containing such an unfriendly sentiment. To please the editor, I changed the poem so that I wished for only a critical injury. The reader will be glad to know that I have restored the original text in this volume.

CONTENTS

LIGHT ARMOUR

MALES

& FEMALES

BIG THREE

Three women regulate my life:
My mother, daughter, and my wife.
At first, when I was not so big,
My mother bent this tender twig.
Then having given me direction,
Advice, admonishment, inspection,
She passed me on to her who wed me
And ever since has loved and led me.
Of late my wife, though still in charge,
Permits the circle to enlarge,
And now my daughter's subtle skills
Augment the older wiles and wills,
For she, by right and by consent,
Is added to the management.
As women's husband, father, son,
I am outnumbered three to one.

IN THE DARK

With woman's persistence, in dead of the night,
My wife does a thing that I've never thought right:
She turns herself over and, head slightly bent,
Comes out with the query, absorbed and intent:
   "You awake?"

She whispers it ever so softly at first,
But once she's been through it and got it rehearsed,
With extra insistence and maybe a twitch
At my bedclothes, she asks in a loftier pitch:
   "You awake?"

If still no response, sitting upright in bed,
And leaning well over and close to my head,
With full blast of lungs and, I think, through cupped hands,
She stubbornly, stridently, sternly demands:
   "YOU AWAKE?"

And I'm forced to admit what I learned long ago:
She isn't amused when my answer is "No!"

TO HAVE AND TOO OLD

The bride, white of hair, is stooped over her cane,
  Her faltering footsteps need guiding,
While down the church aisle, with a wan, toothless smile,
  The groom in a wheel chair comes riding.

And who is this elderly couple, you ask?
  You'll find, when you've closely explored it,
That here is that rare, most conservative pair,
  Who waited till they could afford it.

POT SHOT

My flower-loving wife has lots
Of potted plants around in pots.
She gives them tender, loving care
And moves them here and moves them there
To see that each and every one
Shall have its share of light and sun.

She hikes to distant hill and gulch
To bring them healthy loam and mulch,
She nurses up the tender shoot,
She laves the leaf, bestirs the root,
And frequently large sums invests
In stuff for killing scales and pests.

I do not carp or look askance
Because my wife is kind to plants,
But there is this I'd like to mention:
I wish I got as much attention.

WHAT YOU DON'T KNOW
WON'T HURT YOU TILL LATER

Young man, have you seen her in curlers,
  Have you seen her with face all agleam
With lotions
And potions,
No telling what oceans
  Of cleansing and pore-closing cream?

Young man, have you seen her unpowdered,
  Unrouged on the cheeks and the lips?
Have you eyed
Her untied
And a good bit more wide—
  Ungirdled, I mean, at the hips?

Young man, have you seen her in work clothes,
  In things long outmoded and old,
In slippers
Like kippers
And frocks without zippers,
  Just up from a sniveling cold?

You haven't? Young man, then here's hoping
  Your nerves are as steady as rock.
When you do
Get a view
Of your true love that's true,
  You're in for a helluva shock.

7

MAKE-UP ARTISTS

Women, one finds,
Make up their minds,
Quarrels, and faces
In public places.

AMOR VINCIT OMNIA, BUT NOT, IN THIS
FAMILY, INSOMNIA

I toss and turn for hours on end;
She doesn't stir, she doesn't bend.
I puff my pillow, count my sheep;
She's sunk in deep, refreshing sleep.

I hear the clock beside the bed.
I hear our night-owl neighbor's tread.
I hear each bark in our environs.
She doesn't hear disaster sirens.

And in the morning when, at last,
Into a doze I've somehow passed,
She rouses me to hear her plight:
She hasn't slept a wink all night!

REPEAT PERFORMANCE

A woman never tires of hearing
"I *love* you" said in tones endearing.
She'll hear it when she first gets up,
And then above the breakfast cup,
And yet again, by phone, at noon,
And, dancing, in an off-key croon.
Although she hears it day and night,
She never comes to think it trite.
A man, however, finds this hokum.
Why speak the words, when he just spoke 'em?

DRIVEN TO IT

When I am at the wheel, my frau
Forever tells me what and how,
   And when and if.
But when she's driving, I am still.
I've no remarks about her skill.
   (She scares me stiff.)

YANKEE CLIPPER

My wife, with ever-searching eyes,
Clips recipes she never tries.
She also clips, and promptly loses,
A remedy for sprains and bruises,
A hint on how to take out spots,
And where to keep old flowerpots.
She clips and stuffs away in books
At which, of course, she never looks,
Advice on how to make finesses
And how to press the pleats in dresses
And how to budget, how to plan,
And even how to hold her man.
My wife, her sharpened scissors near,
Clips items out, year after year,
With such a fervent, steady clack,
The gal's a cliptomaniac.

IT TAKES A HEAP O' HAIRPINS

Hairpins on the dresser,
   Hairpins on the floor,
The trail of the possessor
   Leads from door to door.

Hairpins hither, thither,
   Fallen like the rain.
Prepare to slip and slither,
   Step with barefoot pain.

So many are the hairpins
   Scattered everywhere,
One wonders there are spare pins
   Left over for her hair.

LADY, YOUR CLAWS ARE SHOWING

One dreadful truth I rather wish
I did not know is that
The woman who is kittenish
May one day be a cat.

ON THE AVERAGE

Is the driver ahead indecisive?
  Does the car seem to wobble and reel?
I mutter, in accents derisive,
  "There's a woman, of course, at the wheel."

So I drive just a little bit faster,
  To prove what a smart fellow I'm,
And discover I'm right, when I've passed "her,"
  Some fifty percent of the time.

TAKING HER PICK

My wife possessively asserts
Her wifely right to pick my shirts.
With steady hands and birdlike eyes
She picks my hats and socks and ties.
She picks, like other wives and mamas,
My underwear and my pajamas.
She picks my coats, both sport and top,
And there I'd let the matter drop,
Except, as I observe with rue,
She sometimes picks my pockets too.

OFF-THE-CUFF REMARK
ON OFF-THE-SHOULDER DRESSES

Here's one conviction that I hold,
    I've never been in error:
If low-cut dresses leave you cold,
    You're probably the wearer.

ENTICER

A married man who begs his friend,
A bachelor, to wed and end
   His lonesome, sorry state,
Is like a bather in the sea,
Goose-pimpled, blue from neck to knee,
   Who cries, "The water's great!"

MIDDLE AGE

Middle age
Is a time of life
That a man first notices
In his wife.

PAST PERFECT

Wives delight in telling wives
Of the moment in their lives
When, though not exactly lonely,
Bang! they met their one and only.

Husbands, though, among their pals,
Speak more often of the gals
Whom they gave impassioned kisses
Long before they met the Mrs.

LADY SHOPPERS,
BEWARE

Show-window manikins
Have slenderer fannykins.

TEA TOTALER

It now is past six, and since just after three
My wife has been out at an afternoon tea.
For nearly three hours, and with hardly a break,
She's stowed away sandwiches, nibbled at cake,
Tried cheeses and crackers and homemade preserves,
And otherwise padded her generous curves.
But now comes the time for some cooking and carving,
For hubby is home, and the poor guy is starving.

So she, with her appetite jaded and spent,
Bestirs her to cook for the ravenous gent.
With halfhearted effort she opens a can
And listlessly empties it into a pan,
Then having, reluctantly, warmed up some meat
And sliced a tomato (a succulent treat!),
She places a plate in the cramped breakfast nook
And seats herself opposite, reading a book.

To speak for us husbands, I utter a "Fie!"
On afternoon tea (and especially high)
Which, dulling wives' appetites, dulls their incentive
And makes them, at dinnertime, most un-inventive.
I warn you, good ladies, that someday the dike
Of our patience will break, and we'll rise up and strike. . . .
Go walking, go riding, go bridging, but please,
To keep us contented, skip afternoon teas!

CAUTION: WOMAN AT WORK

A woman's dressing table's quite
An awesome and impressive sight,
With bottles full of potent stuffs,
And tweezers, curlers, scissors, puffs,
And brushes, braces, pins, and tubes,
And things in cylinders and cubes,
And jars from which strong odors issue,
And nets and bands and bits of tissue.

So close is its resemblance to
A workman's bench, that I would view
With no alarm if found among
These varied aids for making young
Such other helpful tools of glamour
As saw and plane and wrench and hammer.

HOSTS
& HOSTESSES

GUESTS
& GUESTESSES

GUEST PRIVILEGES

When rare-seen friends come visit us,
   We pull out all the stops.
Though hamburg is our common fare,
   We dine on steaks and chops.

We buy the little costly things
   It's always been a sin to;
Our precious hoard of bottled goods
   Gets quite a going into.

A hired girl brings the dinner in,
   Returns things to their shelves.
We don't know what guests think, but gosh,
   We're quite impressed ourselves!

FRIGHTENING EXPERIENCE

Is this the house? Is this the night?
Did we, my dear, remember right?
No porch light gleams, no one stands near
The windowpane through which we peer.
No cars before the doorway park,
All seems unfestive, still, and dark.
If we should ring, we see ahead
Our host and hostess dragged from bed,
Or he in undershirt, and she
A creamed and curlered sight to see.

With what relief, what brimming cup,
We watch another car drive up
And know, our dreadful fears now gone,
That all is well—the party's on.

BUFFETED

At buffet suppers one has often
But fork or spoon with which to soften
And cut through hunks of ham or turkey
That fight right back, undaunted, perky.
To call for what one needs—a knife—
Would lead to banishment for life;
To eat the meat uncut (no joking),
Would be to run the risk of choking.
One tries to look enthusiastic
While battling gristle—taut, elastic—
And hopes the piece one's sawing through
Gives up before one's muscles do.

THE BACHELOR

The bachelor's a useful man,
Be sure to know one if you can.
He's fine to ask to dinner when
You're just a little short of men.
And when he comes, this chap so handy,
He brings a two-pound box of candy
And, being used to lonesome meals,
Puts on an apron, stirs and peels,
And dinner done, this helpful type
Stays willingly to wash or wipe.
A playful chap, devoid of pomp,
He takes the children for a romp
And tells them tales and, having fed them,
Considers it a lark to bed them.
But here's the puzzling paradox:
Instead of locking all the locks
And pulling shades and barring doors
And keeping him to do her chores,
The hostess cannot wait to choose him
A darling wife, and promptly lose him.

THE PAUSE THAT DEPRESSES

Don't let the conversation lag.
Come on, please, be a wit or wag.
Or if you can't, say something solemn,
Quote from a book, a speech, a column.
Small talk will do, or aimless chatter,
It really, truly doesn't matter.
What makes the hostess pale? Some illness?
Oh, no—a grim, five-second stillness.

HOW WE PLEASE OUR GUESTS

Oh, happy guests, with smiles unfurled,
   Who greet us, having spent the night,
We would not tell you for the world
   Our bathroom scales weigh five pounds light.

IT'S THE SECOND DOOR ON THE LEFT

When we have dinner guests, my wife
    Makes certain that our bathroom,
In case of need, will not look quite
    So like a Grapes-of-Wrath room.

She changes towels, scrubs the tub,
    And carries out the stray things—
The extra shoes, the magazines,
    The children's toys and playthings.

Rare, rare indeed the dinner guest
    Who to our bathroom ambles,
But were there not this constant threat,
    The place *would* be a shambles.

CANDLE POWER

Beneath the subtle candlelight
You ladies *do* look quite all right,
And, seen less clearly, I admit
That I myself improve a bit.

But such the wattage, such the flicker,
Which glass is water, which is liquor?
Is this potato, squash, or rice?
I need a Seeing Eye's advice.

I'd like to know the flowers from
The celery, and not by thumb.
I'd like to know where north and south is,
Or anyhow, just where my mouth is.

For, after all, I came to dine
(And not upon your face or mine),
And so, to find which food is which,
I pray you, please flick on the switch.

THE DISCRIMINATING READER

Beside the guest-room bed I find,
    Placed on a table neatly,
The books my thoughtful host consigned
    To care for me completely:

A tome on migratory birds,
    A treatise on the weather,
A thing on life among the Kurds,
    The *Rubáiyát* in leather,

A Baedeker for Southern France,
    A book for boys by Henty,
A novel that I read, by chance,
    Along in 1920,

A college text in chemistry,
    The Latin odes of Horace,
The prayers of Bertram Blank, D.D.,
    An early Kathleen Norris.

And while I thumb through Eddie Guest
    And blow the dust off Schiller,
What of my host? Propped on his chest
    He holds the latest thriller.

SO SOON?

Our guests are about to go—
The signs, it is true, are small,
But the sensitive host and hostess
Know they'll soon be out in the hall.

Our guests are about to go—
That is, they're all set to start
To plan to prepare to get ready
To begin to commence to depart.

NEVER
THE
TWAIN

Among the friends we entertain
  There are two varied sorts:
The ones who take tomato juice
  And those who like their snorts,

The ones whose talk is quite refined
  And conduct always staid,
And those whose jokes need cleaning up
  And make us pull the shade.

We love them both—the good, the gay—
  They're friends in any weather.
We ask them over frequently,
  But not, if wise, together.

MY FRIENDS ARE SHOWING PICTURES
OF THEIR TRIP

While views are shown of Yokohama
(In front of each stand Sis and Mama),
The docking ship, the loading plane,
The coast of France (or is it Maine?),
A slanting church that's short a steeple,
Some unfamiliar, grinning people,
My face is tilted toward the screen,
A smile upon my lips is seen.
As if entranced, I do not stir,
Contentedly I seem to purr.
And in the dark, few are disposed
To notice that my eyes are closed.

COMMUNICATION SYSTEM

Behind the back of host or guest
　　My wife gives me the high sign—
Instruction, warning, all the rest—
　　By means of hand or eye sign.

She winks, grimaces, jerks her head,
　　And twists at every joint,
While I, with mingled hope and dread,
　　Try hard to get her point.

She registers her fears and pains,
　　Shows histrionic bent,
And afterward, when she explains,
　　I see just what she meant.

LINES THAT WILL NEVER
BE WRITTEN
IN A GUEST BOOK

Your bathroom's nice, its color scheme
   Is one for connoisseurs.
It's always pleasantly agleam—
   And full of you and yours.

You said to make myself at home,
   But hostess, how you kid!
I saw the look upon your face
   The time or two I did.

Your walls are thin, and, on my word,
You'd be surprised at what I've heard.

WHERE THERE'S SMOKE, THERE'S MY FIREPLACE

The kindling's dwindling,
  The log won't catch,
The only blaze
  Is the new-struck match.

The flames are low,
  The smoke is high.
The wood is green
  And so am I.

WEEK-END FLOTSAM

My week-end guests who leave behind
The articles I later find
(The toothbrush and the glasses case,
The hat, the garment trimmed with lace,
The camera, the overshoes,
The bathrobe, bright in many hues)
Should also leave, just as unfailing,
A little cash to cover mailing.

COME ON NOW, BE FUNNY

Before you go, dear week-end guest,
You must endure one final test.
Here is our guest book, pen, and ink—
We'll stand beside you while you think.

However much you'd like to scram,
First coin a golden epigram.
Say something witty, something clever,
Produce a *mot* to live forever.

You say that writing's not your forte?
Come, come, dear fellow, be a sport.
We're waiting with expectant eye
To read before the ink is dry.

If confidence is what you lack,
Peruse this book from front to back.
You'll feel like Shakespeare when you note
The silly stuff the others wrote.

DOCTORED
UP

NEW M.D.

The long, long learning years are past,
   He's feeling all atingle.
He has an office and a nurse:
   There hangs his shiny shingle.

His waiting room is empty still,
   The magazines are tidy.
He opened up on Monday and,
   Well, here it is just Friday.

At last here's what he planned for years,
   He's ready, now, for fees.
He craved a private practice, yes—
   But not *too* private, please!

HOUSE CALL

The patient who lives out on Willoughby Lane
Who phones that she's suffering terrible pain,

The one at the end of the road and beyond,
Whose yard, when it rains, is a quagmire, a pond,

The one with the dog that should be in a pen
But is loose and out looking for medical men,

The patient who lives where you drive and then walk to,
What ails her tonight? She wants someone to talk to.

M.D.s, PH.D.s, D.D.s, & B.V.D.s

Doctors come in many kinds,
    It is a common title.
To name them over, one by one,
    Would be a long recital.

The college prof with Ph.D.
    Called "Mr." is a sad one.
He's never lost a patient, though,
    Because he's never had one.

The preacher is, perhaps, D.D.,
    A pious man of God, he.
But though he's called a doctor too,
    He cares for soul, not body.

While "doctor's" what they call them all,
    Each in his way a gem,
The M.D. is the only one
    They call at three A.M.

CRITERIA FOR NURSES

Doctors like their nurses neat,
With well-washed hands and silent feet.
They like them, if not quite omniscient,
At least well trained, alert, proficient.

Doctors like their nurses steady,
Unflustered, cool, and always ready.
They like them punctual and tireless,
Good-humored, cheerful, ever ireless.

But doctors' wives, as is their way,
At home, imagining, all day,
Hope just one thing, while dusting, cooking:
That hubby's nurse is not good looking.

IDEAL PATIENT

The perfect patient let us praise:
He's never sick on Saturdays,
In fact this wondrous, welcome wight
Is also never sick at night.
In waiting rooms he does not burn
But gladly sits and waits his turn,
And even, I have heard it said,
Begs others, "Please, go on ahead."
He takes advice, he does as told,
He has a heart of solid gold.
He pays his bills, without a fail,
In cash, or by the same day's mail.
He has but one small fault I'd list:
He doesn't (what a shame!) exist.

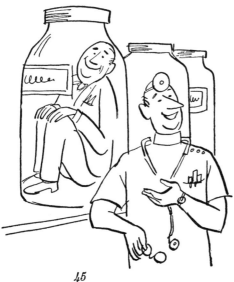

POSTOPERATIVE PUNSTER

Oh, doctor, though you're quite a card,
   You'd sometimes best forget it.
Don't make your patients laugh too hard—
   You may, indeed, regret it.

Withhold those salty tales for men,
   Those puns a bit outrageous;
It ill becomes a doctor when
   His laughter is contagious.

Lay off the funny jokes that tend
   To give them giggling twitches,
Lest patients laugh themselves, my friend,
   Not in but out of stitches.

THE EXTREMELY COMMON COLD

Of all the ills iniquitous,
The cold is most ubiquitous.
It comes to every national,
To sane and to irrational,
To debtor and to creditor,
Illiterate and editor,
To indolent and dutiful,
To ugly and to beautiful,
To modest and to haughty folk,
To pious and to naughty folk,
To high as well as low degree,
To college grad and no degree.
And though you sneeze and cough a lot,
It helps, though not an awful lot,
To know that there's no preference
Regarding colds, or deference,
And even royal highnesses
Have trouble with their sinuses.

ABOUT THE HOUSE

OUR FURNITURE

Our furniture, though fairly decent,
Is far from modern, far from recent.
It's not the kind the stores are selling
Or showing in the model dwelling,
Nor is it something that my wife
Inherited from Duncan Phyfe
Or found, and thereon grew ecstatic,
In some unknowing farmer's attic.
Not really ugly, not quite handsome,
Not worthless, yet not worth a ransom,
The furniture that I discuss
In many ways is much like us.

DEUS EX MACHINA

Or, Roughly Translated, God Only Knows
What Comes Out of the Machine

The kitchen today is so full of appliances,
A cook may get credit for what's really science's.

INSCRIPTION FOR A FLY SWATTER

The hand is quicker than the eye is,
But somewhat slower than the fly is.

MY MATTRESS AND I

Night after night, for years on end,
My mattress has been my closest friend.

My mattress and I are cozy and pally;
There are hills on the sides—I sleep in the valley.

It clearly reveals the shape I'm in:
Where I'm thin it's thick, where it's thick I'm thin.

Its contours reflect the first and the last of me.
It's very nearly a plaster cast of me.

I miss my mattress when I am gone;
It's one thing I've made an impression on.

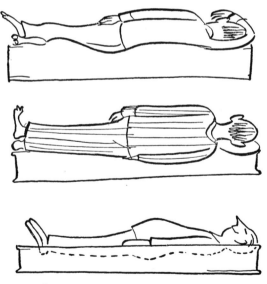

BALLAD OF AN INDOOR FISHERMAN

No fisherman for fish am I,
I don't use either worm or fly,
   Yet fish with might and main.
No seeker out of distant streams
Or lakes on which the sunshine gleams,
   I fish the washbowl drain.

By fishing seasons quite unbound,
I fish and fish the year around
   As fishermen don't dare to.
No limit set upon my catch,
No waiting for the things to hatch,
   I fish all that I care to.

For toothpaste top, for razor blade,
For any object small that's made,
   For cuff link and for ring,
I fish with ice pick and with wire,
With key and pencil (and with ire),
   And gum upon a string.

No fishing hole is more a hole
Than where, intent upon my goal,
   I fish both winter, summer.
And though I catch no bass or trout,
When lucky I am heard to shout:
   "No need to call the plumber!"

ANYBODY HOME?

Salesmen press my doorbell thrice
And then they leave, as meek as mice.
They do not sell me, do not bore,
They set no foot within my door.

Salesmen press my doorbell hard,
But still my door is closed and barred.
I'm not away, I'm right inside.
I move about. I do not hide.

Salesmen press with calloused thumb,
But though I'm there, I do not come.
I read, I snooze, I bathe unirked. . . .
It's years since last my doorbell worked.

"DO YOU PLAY?"

We've a splendid piano, we've had it for years,
And whenever a guest of a sudden appears
We brace for that question—we know he will say
To me or my wife or our kids, "Do you play?"

Now my wife dropped her music, the little she carried,
Some twenty years back, on the day we were married.
My children took lessons, which thoroughly bored them,
Until (lucky youngsters) we couldn't afford them.
And I?—Well, I might have had quite a career
If I'd learned to read music or had a good ear.

And so when we're asked, "Do you play?" by some caller,
We suddenly feel about half a foot smaller.
Afraid to say yes and ashamed to say no,
We learned our stock answer a long time ago.
Our standard reply, noncommittal it's true,
Is always a flattering, friendly "Do you?"

WALLPAPER

Wallpaper comes in many kinds:
The sort that soothes, the sort that blinds,
The kind that strains the strongest eyeballs,
The kind that wiggles after highballs.
It may be filled with ships, with horses,
With lines that follow fancy courses,
With fruit in baskets, ivy, roses,
With dancing girls in frolic poses,
With circles, squares, and candy stripes. . . .
Ah yes, it comes in many types,
And very likely what I'd pick
Would make you just a trifle sick.

ROOM TEMPERATURE

Some hoist the windows, gasp for air,
   While others find it chilly.
Some turn up thermostats a hair,
   While others think them silly.

Some like it cold, some like it hot,
   Some freeze, while others smother.
And by some fiendish, fatal plot
   They marry one another.

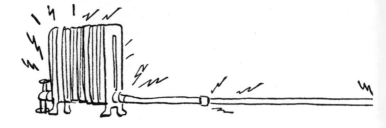

OF PIPES AND PEOPLE

As people grow older, they often grow quiet,
A bit more subdued and less given to riot
    And shrieking and howling and humming.
However the householder's sure to detect
That age has exactly the other effect
    On plumbing.

57

BABY-SITTER BLUES

We're back from the party—it's two A.M.,
    And now can I hit the hay?
Oh no, not yet, for the sitter must get
    To her home, out on Watercress Way.

And so, while my wife toddles off upstairs
    And soon is abed and snoring,
The sitter and I, of the bloodshot eye,
    Set out—and, oh yes, it's pouring.

It's drive across town and over the bridge,
    It's prop up those eyelids of lead,
It's turn up the lane that is soggy with rain,
    It's longing for home and for bed.

It's see that she gets from the car to her door,
    It's wait while she fumbles her key,
It's back by a road the map shouldn't have showed,
    It's home at a quarter past three.

Aye, many the miles to Watercress Way
    And back—and they seem like more.
Oh, let me stay home, when I next would roam,
    Or find me a sitter next door!

SUPPLY PROBLEM

Around our house, where pencils go,
Quite honestly I wouldn't know.
One day the desk has some to spare of them,
The next, it's absolutely bare of them.
Indeed, they disappear so speedily,
I think that someone eats them greedily,
And uses stamps and spare erasers
And rubber bands and clips for chasers.

DESK JOB

The bills for water, gas, and lights
Lie on my desk for days and nights.
One day I have no cash, and then
I have no checkbook, have no pen.
One day I have no envelope,
Another, though I peer and grope,
I have no stamps, or one or two
Cut out of letters, lacking glue.

At last the checks are signed, dispatched,
My desk is clean, my joy unmatched.
The mailman takes the stuff away
And brings me, on the selfsame day,
What drags me down from happy heights:
New bills for water, gas, and lights.

59

BATHTUB COMPLAINT

No singer in bathtubs, I lift up my voice
Against a contraption that gives me the choice
Of sitting bolt upright and warming my knees
While my chest and my back and my upper parts freeze,
Or dunking the top of me, fore part and aft,
And exposing my legs and my feet to the draft.
In short, I'm too long, and I can't for the soul of me
Submerge, as I'd like, at one moment the whole of me.
So I shift back and forth and unhappily fidget
And swear that the tub was designed by a midget.

IN A LATHER

One of the things that I've tried quite hard,
   But still haven't managed to cope with,
Is the cake of soap that's too thick to discard,
   But a little too thin to soap with.

EVEN TENOR OF MY WAY

Though my singing in the bathtub
   Isn't resonant or rich,
And I can't remember lyrics
   And am often off the pitch,

I continue tra-la-la-ing
   And shall do so evermore,
For I've found it very useful
   With no lock upon the door.

PLEASE GRADUATE!

Get in and study, Junior, please,
   And skip a grade or two.
Though I'm not fond of prodigies,
   I cherish your I.Q.

Obey the teacher, break no rule,
   And speed the blessed day
When you will graduate from school
   And I from P.T.A.

MY TEMPERATURE IS UP

My children, when it's hot, wear sweaters
Despite the urging of their betters,
And though they get a look of loathing
Load up with every sort of clothing.

My children, when it's rather chilly,
Are clad so skimpily it's silly,
And when there's winter in the air
Delight in going nearly bare.

My children either aren't so cold
Or hot as those a bit more old,
Or else they need some gentle pats
To jog their sticking thermostats.

SWEEPING STATEMENT

My wife, with scarf around her head
   And madness in her eye,
Upsets the house and me, her spouse,
   And puts the place awry.

I lift my feet, I dodge, I cringe,
   I shift from chair to chair.
I cough and sneeze and wildly wheeze
   Amidst the dust-filled air.

I swept her off her feet, I did,
   Back in those days divine.
Now, room to room, with busy broom,
   She sweeps me off of mine.

MODEL HOME

Out in the newest section,
　　There stands the Model Home.
It's Open for Inspection
　　And glittering with chrome.

Observe the wainscot gleaming,
　　Set foot on well-waxed floors,
And see the salesmen beaming
　　Beside the smudgeless doors.

The fireplace holds no ashes,
　　No soot makes black the edge,
No cobwebs cling to sashes,
　　No dust is on the ledge.

Behold the realtor's pennants,
　　And newly seeded loam. . . .
It takes a lack of tenants
　　To make a Model Home.

BREAKFAST NOOK

We breakfast in a breakfast nook,
    A narrow niche with benches.
To enter it, we twist and crook
    And give our spine some wrenches.

Then, having edged and wedged ourselves,
    Before you can say Finnegan
There's need for stuff on distant shelves—
    We're in, we're out, we're in again.

Our breakfast nook's a useful thing
    That took but little timber,
And while it's fine for breakfasting,
    It also keeps us limber.

GOING TO EXTREMES

Shake and shake
    The catsup bottle.
None will come,
    And then a lot'll.

CHEST EXPANSION

Is my finger bleeding and cut nearly off?
In my medicine chest there's a cure for a cough.

Is a tooth shooting pains out in every direction?
Here is something that's good for a hang-nail infection.

Have I poison ivy, and need for a lotion?
Well, here, all unused, is a seasick potion.

My medicine chest's never known to fail me—
It's bursting with cures for what doesn't ail me.

CHANGE OF ADDRESS

It's true, my children, we used to let you
    Draw pictures upon the wall.
We didn't scold and we didn't fret you
    For racing on skates in the hall.

We didn't mind when in pell-mell play
    The doors were splintered and dented.
But that, my children, was in the day
    When we lived in a house we rented.

THE OTHER SIDE OF THE FENCE

My neighbor, Herbert, is so neat
His yard's the show place of our street.
His lawn is freshly trimmed and mowed,
He even sweeps his share of road.
No leaf has dropped but he has raked it,
No plant has drooped but he has staked it.
He digs and delves till late at night,
His garden is a lovely sight.
His thumb is green? Well, so is mine,
And if perchance you see no sign
Of cultivation in my yard,
I must admit (and this comes hard)
He has the kind you plant and glean with—
It's envy that *my* thumb is green with.

PROOF OF THE PUPPY

He sharpened his teeth
    On the legs of the table
And left, on the rug,
    His indelible label.

He tested his claws
    On the arms of the chair
And deep in the sofa
    Deposited hair.

And now that he's grown,
    As I frequently grouse,
We've a house-broken dog
    And a dog-broken house.
    71

PEDIGREE

How strange that we
Should stand in awe
Of breeding shown
By tail
And paw,

While unimpressed
By pedigrees
Are cockleburs
And cats
And fleas.

WATCHDOG

We bought him for a watchdog,
　But he mixes up his ends:
He wags his tail at strangers,
　And barks at all our friends.

We got him for protection,
　We thought he'd earn his keep.
But he frightens little children—
　When he isn't fast asleep.

He's very fond of hoboes
　And gypsies and the like,
But nips the friendly postman
　And the newsboy on his bike.

He causes feuds and lawsuits,
　He keeps us tense and grim. . . .
We bought him for a watchdog,
　But *we* keep watch on *him*.

AUTHENTIC ANTIQUE

My wife is fond of fine antiques—
Old pitchers, full of years and leaks,
Old paintings, rather faint and faded,
Old jade, and other items jaded,
Old fire screens with but half a screen on,
Old tables, far too frail to lean on.

Her fondness for such wrecks once made
Me quite unhappy when I paid,
But now I'm glad to have her seek
The cracked and bent and worn and weak.
Perhaps, in view of what's been sold her,
She'll love me more as I grow older.

NO SKELETONS IN OUR CLOSETS

No family skeletons,
Naked or gowned.
In *our* closets ever
Will rattle around.

But don't be too hasty,
Too quick to presume.
It's not lack of scandals,
It's lack of room.

FALL GUY

I study the leaves
    And consider the fall of them.
Shall I rake them up piecemeal
    Or wait till there's all of them?

My wife says the first
    Would be neater. No matter.
As I lean on my rake
    I lean more to the latter.

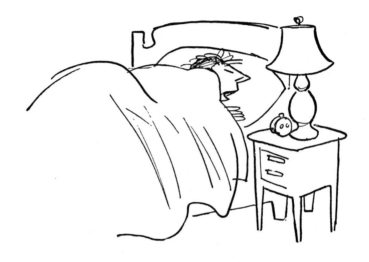

PHILOSOPHY OF A LATE RISER

Day breaks, it's said,
  When night is ended.
I stay in bed
  Until it's mended.

ROOM SERVICE

Breakfast in bed, being pampered and petted,
   You'll have to admit is quite slick.
There's only one trouble: in *our* house, to get it
   You have to be terribly sick.

MEDITATIONS OF A FRUITGROWER

I watch the blossoms coming, going,
   The ever-changing orchard scene.
I watch the season's harvest growing
   And feel the fruitlings, hard and green.

And as I thoughtfully stand under
   The laden boughs, I softly sigh:
Who'll get the crop this year, I wonder,
   The bugs, the birds, the boys, or I?

I SEE
BY THE
PAPER

I DECRY, I DEPLORE

I decry, I deplore, and I righteously score
    The newspaper's love of a story
That's reeking with lechery, murder, and treachery,
    And all that is sinful and gory.

The news that's in fashion is bursting with passion
    It's scandalous, lurid, and gruesome:
The love nest, the gang war, the shoot-'em-dead-BANG war,
    The suicide pact of the twosome.

They print, all the time, every terrible crime
    And perversion you ever have heard of,
The bad, the unlawful, the utterly awful
    I'd not for the world miss a word of.

BEE LINES

Russian experts claim to have trained bees to seek nectar and pollen from specific plants and to ignore others. NEWS ITEM.

How doth the regimented bee
   Improve each shining hour?
He flies to each selected tree
   And designated flower.

The State directs his every course,
   The States defines the sector.
The State prescribes his pollen's source
   And allocates his nectar.

No longer flying fancy-free,
   No longer ranging bold. . . .
How doth the regimented bee?
   He doth as he is told.

LIKE ME, LIKE MY DOG

According to a prominent veterinarian, a nervous master usually has a nervous dog. NEWS ITEM.

Sad thought, that loyal dogs who serve us
May from our nervousness grow nervous,
May even, imitative dummies,
Grow ulcers in their little tummies.
A trembling in our hands may cause
A nervous tic in canine paws,
A strident lifting of the voice
May leave our faithful friend no choice
But somewhat faster, higher yapping
That will disturb our neighbor's napping.
We must be calm, serene all over.
Not just for us—consider Rover.

HARK, HARK, THE THRUSH

A birdwatcher in Texas reports that thrushes are getting drunk from eating too much fruit. They become so tipsy they are unable to fly. NEWS ITEM.

The tipsy thrush, with heavy wings,
Is earthbound as unpinioned things,
And overcome by lush excesses
To stupid flappings retrogresses.

How different the human mammal,
Imbibing like a thirsty camel.
He still can't fly, poor wingless man,
But now at least he thinks he can.

HATS

Hats worn by former Presidents and by famous aspirants to office are included in an exhibition of Presidential campaign materials at the New York Historical Society. NEWS ITEM.

Now on display are stovepipe toppers,
Stiff sailor straws and snap-brim floppers,
Expensive hats of private mintage,
Tired, battered lids of ancient vintage,
Ten-gallon jobs, with brands and x's,
That prove the wearer comes from Texas,
And coonskin caps, as well as derbies,
And hats like FDR's and Herbie's.

Still with us are these famous hats,
Though sat upon by diplomats
And left behind, and changed, with styles,
And waved at cheering crowds for miles
And doffed by breezes, rocks, and eggs,
And chased by aides with limber legs. . . .
These bits of straw and fur and fleece
Have long outlasted war and peace,
Assorted crises, triumphs, boners,
And, come to think of it, their owners.

NUCLEAR MYSTIC

Salvador Dali says he is no longer a surrealist but now a "nuclear mystic." NEWS ITEM.

Surrealism is, to Dali,
Old-fashioned now, considered folly.

The thing to paint's not watches dripping
But atoms, just as they're unzipping,

Or fireballs burning fierce and bright,
Much like the tiger in the night,

Or mushrooms floating in the heavens,
The world at sixes and at sevens,

Or chain reaction broad and bold,
Unlimited and uncontrolled.

All these and other scenes as dizzy
Will, when the master's brush gets busy,

Make Dali's early easel poses
Look like the work of Grandma Moses.

SOME CALL IT PROGRESS

A modern motel has been built in Stratford-on-Avon, down the road a bit from Ann Hathaway's cottage. NEWS ITEM.

The inn is out in Stratford town,
    By Shakespeare's fame exalted.
Motels instead provide the bed
    And malt gives way to malted.

Just down the road from shaded lawns
    That Ann once took her tea on,
Now one may see No Vacancy
    In glowing tubes of neon,

And when they have been guided through
    And finished postcard thumbing,
Tourists may dwell in a motel
    Complete with modern plumbing.

Surpassed by chrome and innerspring,
    The old-time inn is guestless. . . .
Unmoved the stones that guard his bones,
    But Shakespeare's sleep is restless.

DANCE OF THE BEES

The Austrian zoologist Karl von Frisch has shown by a number of careful experiments that bees returning to a hive inform their fellow bees of the distance and direction of a feeding place by means of wagging dances on the comb. Using the sun as a point of reference, they indicate the direction by the angle at which they point in their dance on the vertical comb. FROM AN ARTICLE IN "SCIENTIFIC AMERICAN."

While the drones stand around it and kibitz,
   And the queen gives her queenliest glance,
The worker, returning, exhibits
   Its studied and meaningful dance.

With a bump and a grind and a waggle,
   With a hitch of its hindermost section,
It signals, for fellows who straggle,
   The distance and also direction

To fields where the wild flower burgeons,
   And the blossomy, ripening glades
Where bees, like assiduous surgeons,
   Are probing till sunniness fades.

And meanwhile, in grasses and thickets,
   As honeybees waggle and hop,
The tuneful cicadas and crickets
   Keep time with a kind of bee-bop. . . .

Oh, the sun makes the meadow all spangles,
   And the hive is abuzzing to roam,
As returnees wig-waggle the angles
   In their dance on the vertical comb.

WORD + WORD + WORD + WORD = 𝒑𝒐𝒆𝒎

DISCLOSURE

How can I know what I think till I see what I say? W. H. AUDEN,
IN "POETS AT WORK."

How could the poet
possibly know
till the very last word
in the very last row?

For a poem's a word
plus a word plus a word,
added, subtracted,
and thoroughly stirred.

And thought makes the word
and the word makes thought,
and some things come
that were never sought.

At what he has said
when his say is done,
the poet's surprised
as anyone.

CALCULATED RISK

*Safety Institute Taps the Kitchen as Home's Most Dangerous
Room.* NEWSPAPER HEADLINE.

For safety's sake, let me remind you
That knives can cut and grinders grind you,
That broken glass is left to linger
Upon the sink to slice your finger,
That chairs and stools you reach the wall from
Are really only made to fall from,
That cupboard doors can cave your head in,
And whiffs of gas can leave you leaden,
And fire, if you're a trifle rash,
Can turn you into bone and ash.
Yes, be one careful, be one frisky,
The kitchen is so downright risky,
So perilous to limb and life,
A man best leaves it to his wife.

TRUSTWORTHY

The House of Representatives has voted that American Indians, no longer "hostile or uncivilized," can be trusted with guns.
NEWS ITEM.

The Indian no longer
  Is hostile, as of yore.
His moral sense is stronger,
  He's gentle to the core.

He's through with bow and arrow,
  His knifing days are done.
No longer crude and narrow,
  He's ready for a gun.

Though somewhat slow a starter,
  What progress he has made.
He's set to man a mortar
  And throw a hand grenade.

This change is rather recent,
  It wasn't always thus,
But now he's very decent
  And civilized like us.

THE EMPTY COUCH

Communists have been ordered not to go to psychiatrists for treatment; they have been found to talk too freely under the influence of mental doctors. NEWS ITEM.

Though Communists have furrowed brows
    And eyes with bags and pouches,
They can't relax, they mustn't drowse
    On psychiatric couches.

Libidos must be kept in line,
    Traumatic tilts avoided;
The mental doctor might incline
    To ferret things as Freud did.

Who knows? The chatter might make sense,
    The self might be asserted,
Beneath some subtle influence
    Long-bottled truth be blurted.

Severe the risk, too great by far,
    And so from mental checkup
Are barred the very ones who are
    Most ailing from the neck up.

BE IT EVER SO HOSTILE

*According to the Director of the Association for Family Living,
children should be allowed to be bad at home, since "hostility is
one of the basic emotions and has to be expressed some place."*
NEWS ITEM.

If a lass or a lad
Simply has to be bad,
Because of deep-seated compulsions,
Let it not be at school
Where the mean little fool
Might give the poor teacher convulsions.

Let it likewise not be
Where the neighbors can see
When objects are hurled and broken,
Or at church where the ear
Of the preacher can hear
The horrible words that are spoken.

If a child must rage,
At a certain age,
With hostile emotions atingle,
It's best that he foam
And explode at home,
Says the expert, who's probably single.

HIDING PLACE

A speaker at a meeting of the New York State Frozen Food Locker Association declared that the best hiding place in event of an atomic explosion is a frozen-food locker, where "radiation will not penetrate." NEWS ITEM.

Move over, ham
   And quartered cow,
My Geiger says
   The time is now.

Yes, now I lay me
   Down to sleep,
And if I die,
   At least I'll keep.

MILK OF HUMAN KINDNESS

Cows that feel frustrated or inferior give less milk, according to a member of the University of Minnesota Animal Husbandry Department. NEWS ITEM.

Does Bossie falter, does Bossie fail
To fill to the brim her accustomed pail?
Is production declining, reduced to a trickle,
While hay is now higher by many a nickel?

Don't sell her for short ribs and leather and glue
Till you've done all an owner with honor can do.
There's always the chance she may yet lactate double
If just you can get to the cause of her trouble.

The fault may be yours, or a neighborhood cow's,
That Bossie does nothing but stupidly drowse
And fails to awaken from diffident dreamery
To function at par for the local creamery.

Have *you* been as kind as you should in your dealings?
Have *you,* though unwittingly, injured her feelings?
Have *you* made her life just a little bit drearier
Or snobbishly caused her to feel she's inferior?

A cow is a cow, and yet never forget
That she's also a female, a creature to pet.
So smile when you meet her, stop snapping your galluses,
And arrange for a competent psychoanalysis.

A BALLAD OF ECONOMIC BETTERMENT

According to an official of the Salvation Army, crime among American women has lessened steadily because they have gained economic security. "Nellie doesn't have to sin for pretty clothes any more. If she sins, she has to have a better reason." NEWS ITEM.

Oh, Nellie doesn't have to sin
    For pretty clothes today,
She doesn't have to swig his gin,
    She doesn't have to stray.

She doesn't have to acquiesce,
    Or even slightly sink,
To get herself a party dress
    Or coat of handsome mink.

For Nellie's not dependent, sirs,
    On certain tawdry talents.
She's got a bank account all hers,
    And quite a tidy balance.

No longer does she have to buy
    The things she wants with sex;
She looks the salesgirls in the eye
    And pays her bills with checks.

Today if Nellie sins, you'll know
    It's for a better reason.
It's not that Nellie needs the dough—
    She merely finds it pleasin'!

SHADES OF JOYCE KILMER

Trees Undergo Rigid Tests to Be Telephone Poles.   NEWSPAPER
HEADLINE.

A tree may have the trunk and branch
To do its stuff in yard or ranch,
   May have what it requires
For growing broad and growing big
And sprouting leaves from every twig,
   But not for stringing wires.

A tree may form a roost for birds
And furnish poets fancy words,
   May look the part, no doubt,
Yet though it does its very best
Flunk sadly when it takes the test
   A. T. & T. puts out.

A tree may be correctly made
To bear its fruit and cast its shade
   But fail its final role.
Though only God can make a tree,
He rarely makes it perfectly
   Enough to be a pole.

GUIDED

MISCELLANY

THE ELBOW

The elbow is a sort of hinge;
You bend it when you're on a binge.
You also bend it when you're chancing
A quick embrace, or when you're dancing.
It's like the knee, but in the arm
(And has about as little charm),
And if no good to bounce your daughter on,
It's also what you don't get water on.
It's called the funnybone in fact,
Though nothing's funny when it's whacked.
The elbow's good for giving nudges
To get attention, pay off grudges.
It's used by many, I assume,
For getting what's called elbow room.
Though lacking beauty, it no doubt
Would be quite hard to do without,
And thus is one rough place that gents
Can call a joint without offense.

FISH STORY

Count this among my heartfelt wishes:
To hear a fish tale told by fishes
And stand among the fish who doubt
The honor of a fellow trout,
And watch the bulging of their eyes
To hear of imitation flies
And worms with rather droopy looks
Stuck through with hateful, horrid hooks,
And fishermen they fled all day from
(As big as this) and got away from.

AMBITION

I have the Itch to Get Ahead,
  An itch that's nigh unmatchable.
It's not connected with my skin
But somewhere very deep within,
  And therefore quite unscratchable.

DISTANCE LENDS SOMETHING OR OTHER

I don't wear glasses, but I place
The print some distance from my face,
A distance that increases yearly
If I would read the letters clearly.

I don't wear glasses, though I fear
I'll have to, almost any year.
My eyes, I find, are plenty strong enough;
It's only that my arms aren't long enough.

TRADE-IN ALLOWANCE

Here's how I save hundreds of dollars
   On trade-ins involving my car:
I rub till the dirt and the squalor's
   All gone, and it gleams like a star.

I paint all the spots that are rusted,
   I lovingly hammer out dents,
I fix all the things that are busted,
   I mend all the rips and the rents.

It looks, when I'm through, like a honey,
   Its value goes up with a leap,
And—here's where I really save money—
   It's handsome enough, now, to keep.

SINGING THE BLUES

I have a suit of navy blue,
   In none do I look dandier,
And sport a pocket handkerchief,
Although it is my firm belief
   A whisk broom would be handier.

COIN RETURN

Although I try, I cannot spurn
The place on phones marked "Coin Return."
A strange compulsion makes me linger
And test with probing index finger.

Let me but say to those not bound
By such a habit: I have found
That this exploratory itch
Is not a way of getting rich.

COVERING THE SUBJECT

The turtle, clam, and crab as well
Are covered with a sturdy shell,
While fish, excepting maybe whales,
Are shingled fore and aft with scales.

Though most, perhaps, have not the plating
Of armadillos, it's worth stating
That animals at least have hides
That give them fairly firm outsides.

And yet that upright mammal, man,
Must get along as best he can
With nothing but a little skin
To keep his precious insides in.

THE ANT

The ant, a prodigy of strength,
Lifts objects twice his weight and length
And never stops or sighs or glowers
Because it's after working hours.
Though underground, he bears the onus
And peril without thought of bonus,
And never once is heard to mention
Retiring on a tax-free pension.
Nor does he frown or look askance
At other, lighter-burdened ants.
Not one to bicker, blame, or sob,
Not angling for a better job,
The ant has but one flaw I see,
To wit, he doesn't work for me.

LINES FOR THE DAY AFTER ELECTIONS

The sun still rises in the east,
The song of skylarks has not ceased,
The mountains stand, the seas are calm,
I hear no detonating bomb.

The banks are open, trains on time,
The morning paper's rich with crime,
A stream of traffic fills the street,
The ground is firm beneath my feet.

No cataclysmic conflagration
As yet has swept our luckless nation.
No sign of doom have I detected,
Although my man was not elected.

SO MANY PEOPLE PUT THEMSELVES INTO MY
SHOES THAT I THINK I'LL GO BAREFOOT

My friend says not to worry,
    My friend pooh-poohs my fears.
His words are quite consoling,
    His optimism cheers.

This view unvexed, undaunted,
    How comforting it is. . . .
He looks upon my worries
    The way I do at his.

THE CONSCIENCE

The conscience is a built-in feature
That haunts the sinner, helps the preacher.
Some sins it makes us turn and run from,
But most it simply takes the fun from.

RAIN

Rain that fosters growing plants
Takes the creases out of pants.

Rain that settles summer dust
Causes mildew, causes rust.

Rain that, with its cleansing fall,
Washes autos, makes them stall.

Rain that fills the dried-up creek
Causes people's roofs to leak.

Rain that cools you when it's hot
Makes you shiver when it's not.

Rain's a mixed-up sort of weather,
Pro and con all rolled together.

Rain is nasty, rain is nifty,
In proportion, fifty-fifty.

THE WEATHERMAN

Consider calmly, if you can,
The weather-beaten weatherman.
If he says rain and it is sunny,
We ridicule him, think it's funny.
If he says fair and skies are grim,
Our day is spoiled, and we blame him.
If he says fair and fair's the clime,
We say we knew it all the time.
Although he charts his highs and lows
And studies figures ranged in rows
And telephones a friend long-distance
And checks with capable assistants
And takes a final, hurried glance,
He knows he doesn't have a chance.

LIBRARY

Here is where people,
    One frequently finds,
Lower their voices
    And raise their minds.

A PLAGUE ON BOTH YOUR HOUSMANS

When I was one and twenty
  And first went to the polls,
Oh, I was thrilled aplenty
  To be upon the rolls.

I sang a little song, then,
  I did a little dance.
I knew the right from wrong, then,
  I knew it at a glance.

But now I'm somewhat older,
  I've grown a trifle gray,
And now my zeal is colder
  Upon election day.

The dimming of my sight, lads,
  I might perhaps endure,
But as for wrong and right, lads,
  I wish I could be sure!

Wordsworth, who was fairly mild,
Had an illegitimate child.
Coleridge almost all his life
Yearned for someone not his wife.
Shelley, an amoral elf,
Caused his wife to drown herself.
Byron, who was most tempestuous,
Went the limit, was incestuous.
Keats, who might have had the gumption,
Was retarded by consumption.
Rarely did the great Romantics
Equal, in their verse, their antics

A LITTLE LEARNING

A little learning is a pleasant thing,
A modicum of knowledge do I sing.
Not such a very little as may shame us
And set us down a vulgar ignoramus,
Nor yet the heavy freight of special lore
That causes us to lose the friends we bore.
A few not soon forgotten dates will do,
Such as for instance 1492;
We do not need the month or day or whether
Columbus had the proper sailing weather.
Sufficient information about art
To tell the Vans, both Dyke and Gogh, apart,
But not to detonate like a torpedo
When others don't pronounce Van Gogh as we do.
A little learning saves us grief and labors,
Just so it's not so little as our neighbor's.

BACK-TO-NATURE WRITER

In books and articles he hymns the pleasures
  Of simple, golden days of long ago.
He quotes at length, and obviously treasures,
  Bucolic thoughts of Wordsworth and Thoreau.

He sometimes grieves, he sometimes shouts defiance
  At man too mechanized, enthralled with chrome.
Deploring deeds of industry and science,
  He writes of rustic woodlands as his home.

But do not shed for him a tear of pity
  Or hasten by his written word to judge him.
He lives where born, amidst a bustling city
  From which a team of horses couldn't budge him.

LINES LONG AFTER POPE,
BY A READER OF FRESHMAN THEMES

Small wit is theirs, in shopworn phrases dressed;
What oft was thought, and twice as well expressed.

TWENTY-FIFTH REUNION

Well, here we are, with husbands and with wives,
Accounting for the passage of our lives,
Remembering the good old good old days
And singing good old Alma Mater's praise
And smiling and exchanging commonplaces
While trying hard to bracket names and faces.
New, unfamiliar buildings frame the Quad,
But these are not so startling, not so odd
As what abrasive years have done to hair
And teeth and such. Oh, no, we mustn't stare,
We mustn't start, or grow the slightest teary
But only slap the stooping back and query
"How many children have you?" "What's your line?"
And always comment on the answer, "Fine!"
The bald wear hats, the ones with dentures hold
Their lips a trifle tight, the fat ones fold
The flesh in so that it won't be apparent. . . .
Be kind, we tell ourselves, and be forbearant,
And afterward let not a moment pass:
Go home and look into the looking glass.

THOSE CLEVER RUSSIANS

One thing that some Russian, completely demented,
I'm willing and glad to acknowledge invented
Is Russian roulette, a brave game that is said
To be played with a pistol that's placed at your head.
It's a matter of luck if the chamber is loaded,
You'll know that it is when the gun has exploded.
It's clever, it's Russian, it's sure to repay you.
And fun? It not only will please you, but slay you!

GOSSIPS' END

When gossips die, as mortals must,
    And leave their earthly home,
Their punishment will be, I trust,
    Eternally to roam

Down dismal paths and darkened pits
    And empty halls of hell,
With heads crammed full of juicy bits
    And not a soul to tell.

ABOUT THE AUTHOR

Richard Armour is a Dr. Jekyll and Mr. Hyde. As the serious, scholarly Dr. Jekyll he is a Harvard Ph.D., holder of research fellowships in England and France, author of books of biography and literary criticism, and longtime professor of English at such institutions as the University of Texas, Northwestern University, the University of Freiburg, the University of Hawaii, Wells College, Scripps College, and the Claremont Graduate School. He has also lectured in Europe and Asia as an American Specialist for the State Department.

As the fiendish (but more playful) Mr. Hyde he has contributed thousands of pieces of light verse and prose to the leading magazines of the United States and England and has written numerous books of humor and satire on such subjects as history (*It All Started with Eve, Our Presidents,* etc.), literature (*The Classics Reclassified, American Lit Relit,* etc.), medicine (*It All Started with Hippocrates* and *The Medical Muse*), golf (*Golf Is a Four-Letter Word*), adolescence (*Through Darkest Adolescence*), and education, (*Going Around in Academic Circles* and *A Diabolical Dictionary of Education*). His many books for children range from *A Dozen Dinosaurs* to *On Your Marks: A Package of Punctuation,* the latter recently released as an animated film. Some of his adult books are in prose and some are in verse; all of his children's books are in verse and full of playful rhymes and meters.

Richard Armour is married, has a son and daughter, and lives in Claremont, California.

ABOUT THE ARTIST

Tennessee-born Leo Hershfield, illustrator of innumerable books and articles, has traveled far and wide (he has just returned from Nigeria, as a matter of fact, on an assignment for the State Department). His travels have covered New York City (where he studied at the Art Students League and worked for *The New York Times* and other papers), Washington (where he sketched Senate filibusters), Dallas (where he portrayed the Ruby trial), and various sketching tours for television. He lives in Florida, where he has time for such hobbies as sailing, painting watercolors, and reading Richard Armour, this being the sixth of his books he has illustrated.

Catalog

If you are interested in a list of fine Paperback
books, covering a wide range of subjects
and interests, send your name and address,
requesting your free catalog, to:

McGraw-Hill Paperbacks
330 West 42nd Street
New York, New York 10036